Secret Sins

by

Dilla (Ree) Scott

DORRANCE
PUBLISHING CO
EST. 1920
PITTSBURGH, PENNSYLVANIA 15238

The contents of this work, including, but not limited to, the accuracy of events, people, and places depicted; opinions expressed; permission to use previously published materials included; and any advice given or actions advocated are solely the responsibility of the author, who assumes all liability for said work and indemnifies the publisher against any claims stemming from publication of the work.

Dorrance Publishing Co
585 Alpha Drive
Suite 103
Pittsburgh, PA 15238
Visit our website at *www. dorrancebookstore. com*

ISBN: 978-1-4809-1198-7
eISBN: 978-1-4809-1520-6

0 Ps. 122: 6: "They shall prosper that love thee."

Reference: Genuine KJV Bible

Dedicated to, all abused children.

Ruth 2:4: "The Lord be with you."

I want to thank my children: Alfred(A1), Angelleana (A2), Alexander(A3), my therapist with Oasis, and my Esther Sisters KJV (the name means star), for supporting my obedience to God, in the writing of this book. Thank God, for Friend's Ministries, in Lake City Mi., for the garden. All glory to God!!!

In the name of Jesus; my God, how I do love thee. Ps. 122:6 "They shall prosper that love thee." My goal is to tell of Jesus' victory over abuses done to me, and to let you know; Jesus, is your victory. 2 Corinthians 3-4: "Blessed be God, even the Father of our Lord Jesus Christ, the Father of mercies and the God of all comfort. 4. Who comforteth us in all our tribulation, that we may be able to comfort them which are in any trouble, by the comfort by wherewith we ourselves are comforted of God."

The Holy Spirit is writing a book through me. Praise the Lord. All glory to God!!!.

Whenever one member of a family is abused, the entire family is abused. Therefore, I try not to mention my mother or, my siblings. I often think of the day mamma told me of the old Southern tradition of giving the first born girl, to the man of the house, I told her that was stupid. The day A1, stood by me and influenced me to ask her; if she knew that daddy had sexually abused me, was very significant. That's the day I stopped feeling terrifyingly intimidated by her. I am blessed A1, A2, and A3 are non-supportive of abuse. Charity starts at home. 1 Corinth. 13:1 & 13 and 14:1. Though I speak with tongues of men and of angels, and have not charity, I am become as sounding brass, or a tinkling cymbal. 13. And now abideth faith, hope, charity, these three; but the greatest of these is charity. 14. Follow after charity, "(love). Charity starts at home. May God, be with us all.

In the name of Jesus; thank you God, for your many blessings seen and unseen. Thank you God, for Jesus Christ as my savior. Thank you for The Holy Spirit, and the guidance in what to do and what to say. Most of all, thank you for You. This is how I've started my day, for many years. I think on these words throughout the day while doing whatever I am doing. They penetrate my heart, mind, body, and soul. They uplift me. I start my day by enjoying my creator's love, by acknowledging his presence, and by giving Him the first of me every morning. I have faith he is going to give me himself all day. This is how I start my flow of blessings. I have a hunger and thirst for God. During the good times and the bad times, I praise and thank him. I depend on, my Abba (Daddy) Father's strength. Isa. 12:2: "the Lord JEHOVAH is my strength and my song." I have been running after God, for over fifty years. I can never know enough about him. God, is my true love. I also, asked God; to bless me to bring His children to Him. For about five years, his response has been for me to write a book. Now I understand why. As Jesus' spirit in me will be infinite throughout His, book. I pray others will endure my testimony to strengthen their walk with, Jesus. Nehemiah 13:2 "howbeit our God, turned the curse into a blessing." In blessing others, I will be blessed. You are reading this book, so I have faith that you are being blessed. God, has blessed me to let his word live in my heart,

4

mind, and soul. Just as He has blessed you, as you love, Him. God promises; Hebrew 13:5: "I will never leave thee, nor forsake thee." Lying is a sin. Only God is perfect and does not lie to us. Numbers 23:19: "God is not a man that He should lie." I have faith that everyone reading this book will be blessed to see Jesus' love beyond any and all abuse they are experiencing, or have experienced. 1 John 4:16: "And we have known and believed the love God hath to us. God is love; and He that dwelleth in love dwelleth in God, and God in him."

I was four or five years old when I first handedly, unknowingly witnessed the devil, attack me Eph. 6:12: "For we wrestle not against flesh and blood, but against principalities, against powers, against the rulers of the darkness of this world, against spiritual wickedness in dark places." The devil has numerously attacked Jesus through me. However, Jesus declared victory on Calvary, when He said, "it's done," and the veil in the tabernacle was rent in twain. This means right there, and then Jesus defeated satan.

One day, at the age of four, a neighborhood boy and I were playing house, and one of my siblings just so happened to catch us playing husband and wife. We were only touching and rubbing on one another. My sibling promised he wouldn't tell. He kept his word, but every time my brother looked at me I was begging him not to tell. I eventually got caught begging him not to tell, and had to tell on myself. I was made to stand on one foot in a corner of mamma and daddy's bedroom for hours, as they stared at me in conversation with one another. Daddy looked perversely happy. That's the day I remember seeing that evil deceitful look in his eyes. Thats the day I remember becoming his prey, and he became my abuser. This was my beginning of a generation curse of abuse. I have often wondered why did, God, give me to my parents. Maybe it was so that one day, I could tell His children about His graceful love. The abused does not have to be an abuser. Proverbs 11:17: "The merciful man doeth good to his own soul: but he that is cruel trouble his own flesh." My daddy was narcissistically self righteous. He paid the bills. He bought what we needed. He also, kept a roof over our heads. The biblical meaning of fear is to have reverence for. I did not respect him. I was scared of him. I fear(respect) and reverence God. After years of mental and emotional turmoil, I have come to the conclusion that he made his own rules. He seemed to admire himself more than he did God. He was not a reflection of, Abba

(Daddy) Father. Jesus, took me pass and beyond my earthly daddy's hatefulness. I chose to see Jesus' love. I Am God, has always told us how to treat one another. God has chosen to love his children since the beginning of time. We have to choose to accept, process, and reciprocate his love in order to be the best we can be. Molestation and rape is hate, not love. It's evil. Psalms 34:21 "Evil shall slay the wicked: and that they hate righteousness shall be desolate." Jesus, flipped hate. 1 Corinth. 13:4: "charity suffereth long, and is kind." Sometimes actions speak louder than words. 1 John 3:10-11 10: "In this the children of God are manifest, and the chil-

dren of the devil: whosoever do not righteousness is not of God, neither he that
loveth not his brother. 11. for this is the
message ye heard from the beginning, that
we should love one another." Abuse of any
kind, is not love. My earthly father's only
admirable attribute was his work ethics.
He worked every day and did not miss a
day from his job, unless he felt it was an
emergency. He worked the same full time
job for over 40 years, before retiring. He
kept his family out of the ghetto. He sometimes worked one or two additional part
time jobs "to keep his family out of the
ghetto," of which mamma constantly reminded me. Mamma was a stay at home

mom. We had her parents, Mother-dear and Grand-daddy. They loved us. Daddy's family had very little involvement in our lives. Daddy tried to progress beyond his sixth grade education. He said; he just could not learn (a sign of abuse). I was not allowed to socialize with peers or neighbors. I lost my freedom and was a hidden victim due to his acts of molestation, which triggered ostracization by some of my family members. When we lived on Ada, daddy's favorite place was he and momma's bedroom. When she left the house, he often forced me to get into bed with him while some of my siblings were left on the other side, banging on the bedroom door, hollering and crying to come in. He ignored them. He would tell me, "No," when I asked if they could come in. I hated the feeling of them being unprotected and alone. When mamma was gone, she expected me to take care of them. He always demanded my attention and he cared less about leaving them left alone. I hated his touch. I hated to look at him. I quietly hated him, for a long time. I dare not to let him know it because, he might stop taking care of the seven of them. There was mamma, 6 other siblings, and myself (one of my siblings lived with motherdear and granddaddy)]. I wanted to be rid of my earthly father. I wanted to play and have fun with my siblings. It seems I was only allowed to play with them when I was playing mamma to them because, daddy wanted to play house with me as if they were our children. I wanted to love them as a sister, not as a mother. I was accused of being his favorite child, when all the time he was secretly being mean to me. He was fondling me or making me fondle him. I did not want him to touch me. Even though I hated everything about him, the beatings and threats kept me quiet. Upon my acceptance of Jesus as my savior, each time he came near me, Jesus would cuddle me in his arms and endure all of the pain that was meant for me.

I felt nothing. I was unknowingly surrendering all to Jesus, as a child. I learned to have agape love for him, even though I will always hate his letting the wicked spirits attack me through him. Sometimes, daddy gave me money, or said he was going to buy things for my siblings and I, and I believe this was a manipulation to keep me quiet. I was taught to share everything with my siblings. We were solely dependent on him. One day since we have become adults, I tested one of my siblings. I wanted to know how much he/or she would share with me. I had years prior donated 10% of a settlement to one of his/her ventures. I've always tried to help whenever one of them asked me to. I asked for a $40.00 loan, and was turned down. I've since come to realize my sibling had a right to say no. The word "no" was not a part of my vocabulary. My dad and mom did not allow me to say no. Jesus let me know that my daddy would have to answer to him. Gen. 42:22: "Do not sin against the child." That child's name is, Ree. She somewhere along the way hid within me as I grew up. She became introverted, and played the adult role placed upon her Nahum 1:2: "The Lord revengeth and is furious, the Lord will take vengeance on His adversaries, and He reserveth wrath for his enemies." I was an adult with grown children of my own, when I realized how healthy it can be to say, "no". However, I have never had a problem accepting the word, no. I better have accepted it, or I got beat. As I reflect on the cruelties Jesus endured for me, I am extremely happy He loves me. I sometimes got beat because I was told I looked like my dad, or my siblings did something wrong when I was taking care of them. I got beat so much, until sometimes one of my siblings took the blame to take a beating for me, of which I paid for. That same sibling committed incest on me, of which I told his ex-wife about before she met him. Anyhow, years prior, one day, my dad was bottle feeding one of my younger siblings. We used glass bottles back then. The bottle fell. I did not know the floor was covered with glass. Daddy had told me to hold my sibling. I wanted to play. I was a child and I was tired of always giving up what Ree needed and (or) wanted. I wanted to play. Anyhow, I laid my sibling on the couch. He/she rolled onto the floor. The wound on his/her arm was huge. My sibling was only maybe three months old. Blood gushed out. Daddy took care of him/her and chased me from one room to another for what seemed like hours. He literally beat the skin off of my back. As a matter of fact, I was not allowed to wear shorts or short skirts as a little girl, young lady, or etc. Mom said; ladies did not wear shorts and skirts pass one inch above the knees. About four years ago, my children asked me about the scars on my legs. I then realized, mom made me wear the apparel necessary to keep the physical scars hidden. I have always looked past the scars on my legs, just as I have the black eyes I received while intervening to keep my mom from being beaten so badly. A doctor once asked me what happened to my eyes. I told him as mom had told me, that I am a nemic. He told me that was not true. He said; my eyes are black from constantly getting hit in them. After a long hard look in the mirror, I remember the beatings that caused physical cuts and bruises, and left me scarred. All of these years I thought I was being taught not to be disrespectful in the way I dressed, but I was being taught to hide evidence of abuse. Yet, there are no scars on my knees. I use to cut my knees with a razor. I then thought I could get rid of the dry darker skin. I've recently learned that I was cutting myself to feel something other than the pain I was being subjected to. I still do not use the abuses done to me as an excuse to be mean to hurt, or mistreat others. I am still giving it all to Jesus. Especially the forgotten pain from regained memories. I know God loves me.

Hos. 14:4: "I will love them freely;" Num. 23:19: "God is not a man that he should lie." I choose to use the assaults to my soul, body, mind (and), or spirit for the glory of God. Esther 9:22: "turned on them from sorrow to joy." Jesus bore everything for me. Through daddy's wickedness, I experienced Jesus' security of love. I actually saw Jesus face as He held me in His arms. I saw tears run down His face as He endured pain meant for me. I don't remember fighting daddy. I laid motionless and concentrated on Jesus' love for me. 2 Cor. 5:14: [A1's(my first born) birth date is 5/14] "The love of Christ constraineth us. Daddy spent many years suffering with stomach ulcers. He, used me every chance he got. I had to miss school or child-play to clean house, wash clothes, change diapers, cook, be molested, or whatever else. I was at daddy's mercy. He was the head of his household. I used to clean so much until some of my siblings called me, Hazel. I pray daddy chose Jesus in his heart, prior to his death. Whether he knew it or not, he has always had Jesus' mercy. 2 Sam. 24:14: "For his mercies are great." Acts 22:16 "wash away thy sins, calling on the name of the Lord." I was recently told by one of my siblings that one of my uncles said: molestation was a way of life, down generations, against the females in our family. I plead the blood of Jesus, against that generation curse. Jesus, has the power to send that evil, wicked spirit back to where it came from and believe it is burning in the eternal fire in hell, right now. No more, no more, no more, in the almighty name of Jesus; it's done. Momma's parents, Grand-daddy and Mother-dear, were second parents to us. They lived on Ada Street, two blocks away from us. Through them I saw a life I dreamed for. Mother-dear or Grand-daddy sometimes picked us up on Fridays, while on their way from work. We spent many weekends with them. What a delightful change. I was not allowed to visit or spend the night anywhere else. There was no hollering, fighting, arguing, cursing or molestation. There was an atmosphere of peace at their house. They were a real life couple, that chose not to hurt others. I wanted to have a marriage like Grand-daddy and Motherdear, {the Huxtable's (from the Bill Cosby Show)}. I have always wanted my children to have a better life than I did. I wanted to be a good example to them like Grand-daddy and Mother-dear were to me. Up until the day Grand-daddy died, he had nothing to do with my earthly daddy(LS). He did not allow LS, in his house. Grand-daddy never violated me. I never saw him hit or abuse anyone, and he was healthy and strong. He obviously had boundaries of love. Jesus is my hero and Grand-daddy is my earthly mentor. We didn't spend very much time with LS parents or his siblings. Mother-dear normally went pass or stopped at our house every day, on her way home from work if only to say hi and check on us. We occasionally went to church with Mother-dear. At approximately seven years of age, during one of those services, I accepted Jesus Christ as my Lord and Savior. I have not been alone since that moment. Jesus has become my best friend. Through the Holy Spirit and the Bible, Jesus talks with me, Judges me, forgives me, corrects me of my mistakes, and guides me through trials and tribulations. He tells me what to say and do. Eph. 6:18: "Praying always with all prayer and supplication in the spirit, and watching thereunto with all perseverance and supplication for all saints." Ps. 27:1: "The Lord is the strength of my life,"

I was fourteen years old when I started working summer jobs with the goal of buying my school necessities. Momma changed my age to 16 for the job. I paid rent, and did what I could for my siblings without falling helpless to daddy. At the age of sixteen, right after daddy had penetrated me, he asked me if I minded what he was doing to me. I wanted to scream and castrate him. I believed saying yes would get me a beating. With a motionless body and heart so cold that I felt the chill. I heard the Holy Spirit tell me to say no. As hard as it was to be obedient, I softly said; no. That was the last day daddy physically touched me.

During my freshman year of high school I dated, G. H., He dropped me and dated someone else, because I would not have sex with him. The following year, I heard they had a child together. I really believed I could save myself for my husband, because it would have been the first time I would have willingly intimately touched or been touched by a man. He use to buy me beautiful gifts. My mom would either take them from me or made me give them back. She said; I was not for sale. I often wonder was this she or daddy's idea or both. I refused to let him manipulate me into having sex with him. I believed I could be healed of all the abuse that had been done to me. I also knew I had to empty the garbage that crept into my soul, and I had to replace it with Jesus' love for me. GH kept trying to be with me, so I transferred schools at the beginning of my junior year. I went from Simeon to CVS. I did not want to be around him. For two years I majored in commercial Arts. I loved that class. Momma kept my portfolio for many years, and gave it to me in 199?. Years later, I lost it while relocating to Chicago, or moving back to, Michigan. When my children were young, they often talked about how much they loved the art in that portfolio. The most treasured item I lost in moving was a family bible that Mother-dear, gave me. While giving it to me, she said that my mother had given it to her in 1956, the year that I was born. Anyhow, I met S. B. in, Commercial Arts. S. B. and I became best friends. We started hanging out together. We use to say we were bobbsey twins. She was a change from two girls I had met in eighth grade. They appeared to be nice girls. They were good friends to one another. I thought we all had accepted one another as friends. For our first Christmas as friends, we were supposed to buy each other gifts. I spent the only money I had left on them, after buying my siblings gifts. The gifts did not cost a lot of money. They could have bought me a piece of bubblegum, and I would have been happy. They bought me nothing. They laughed at me. I did not try to have friends, again. S. B. , and my common denominator was art, and we became genuine friends. She or I never hurt one another on purpose. S. B. , and M. C. were dating during high school. After graduating from High School they introduced me to M. J. , one of M. C.'s friends. M. J. and I started dating.

One evening, I was half an hour late coming home from a date, with M. J. I got home at 10 P. M. instead of 9:30 P. M. The next day, mamma attacked me, and evicted me from daddy and her house. I was tired of the beatings. I was tired of being called obnoxious names like slut, whore, and bitch. None of those descriptions fitted me. I had never willingly slept with anyone. I yearned to be pure for my husband. I did not fight back. I refused to disrespect my parents. Epes. 6:2: "Honour thy father and mother." I wanted my God to be proud of me. I called S. B. , and she helped me. She did not let me become homeless, even though I cracked D. B. , her brother in the head one day for inappropriately touching me. I lived with her and her aunt's family for a while. When her mom (S. L.), moved her family into their home, she let me move in. S. B.'s family, loved me and I knew it. They were kind and mercifully empathetic even though they did not know the circumstances causing me to live with them. They extended their home to me. To S. B. and her family, I will always be grateful. Those were some of the best years of my life. In 2011, I found out S. L., had gone home to glory in 2009. I had lost touch with S. B. and her families. One of her sisters had divorced one of my brother many years prior. Not even one of them told me S. L. had died. I lost touch with almost everyone in Chicago, when I moved to Michigan. While living with S. B.'s family, I self-learned English penmanship, and sentence structure under the demand of, The Holy Spirit. I was lacking verbal and written etiquette, as well as articulation. I use to write heart wrenching poems. I lost them. I was determined to learn acceptable and enjoyable communication skills. I've had a desire to capture God's, children's attention with, testimonies of His truth, for His glory. I thought I was going to write poems. I never imagined that God, would tell me to write a book for him. Jn 8:29: "Do those things that please Him." Dt. 32:4: "He is the rock. His work is perfect: for all His ways are judgement: a God of truth and without iniquity, just and right is He."

After attending Kennedy King College, I decided to work. There was no problems at SL's house. She was, independent, loving, and nurturing. She chose not to be dependent on a man. After a couple of years of dating M. J. , I miscarried our child. He told me; that if I did not marry him, he would leave me. I loved him and we were good together. We got married at S. L.'s house. I did not invite my dad and was glad he did not attend. M. J.'s family came. M. J.'s dad owned his own trucks. M. J. drove one of them. I was then working in the insurance industry. M. J. and I had moved into our own apartment, and had ordered a lipstick red and gray Thunderbird, exactly the way we wanted it. M. J. started falsely accusing me of having an affair. He became abusive by choking me. G. H. , approached me one day, while I was with M. J.'s sister and her best friend. I wouldn't talk with him. I was committed to M. J. I stayed faithful to him regardless to the abuse. Each time M. J. choked me, he burnt some of the skin off of my neck.

I had accumulated a scarf to match every outfit. One day, he burnt every piece of skin from my neck. I ran out of the apartment building. He ran behind me shooting his gun. I hid behind cars, as I prayed not to be seen or get caught by him. I still loved him, but I had vowed I would never remain in an abusive relationship. I had never committed adultery. I ran to my sister-in-law's house. A. C. , was there and became my, Prince Charming. However, not even he could take my king's place. You know my king. His name is Jesus. I so want a man to love me like Christ loves the church. A. C. , was kind. He doctored my wounds. I slept and rested for a couple of days. When I went to see my family's doctor, she could not believe M. J. , had used his bare hands. I could not believe he would hurt me and yet said; he loved me. I believed we were going to be married forever. Col. 3:19 "Husbands, love your wives." We were going to grow old together. We were going to be like Granddaddy and Mother-dear. When he started choking me, he ruined my desire to be with him. I later found out M. J. had impregnated someone else. I sadly divorced MJ. I hate divorce." Matt. 19:7-8: "7. They say unto him, Why did Moses then command to give a writing of divorcement, and to put her away? "8. He saith

unto them, Moses because of the hardness
of your hearts suffered you to put away
your wives: but from the beginning it was
not so." I wanted to choke him. He ruined
my dreams for us. Oh well, life has to go
on. Papa (daddy's father), told me to keep
trying until I got it right. Over one and a
half years of getting to know A. C. , I
again fell in love. A. C. had tried to get me
to commit bigamy. I almost did. My divorce came a couple days before marrying
A. C. . Just in time. We flew to Virginia, to
be embraced by A. C.'s, family. One of my
siblings and his wife were there. This sibling once told me marrying your sibling
was permissible in other countries. A. C.'s

aunt, uncle, and their neighbors gave us a beautiful wedding. A. C. had written a song to me. I remember it to this day. We received so much love, and some beautiful presents. It was a fairytale wedding. We returned home to our apartment in Chicago, to enjoy a peaceful life full of love. So, I thought. I had to eventually accept the reality that, A. C. was a whore monger. We both had come from dysfunctional homes. One major difference was that A. C. had great control over his anger. So, I thought. In all actuality, he controlled his emotions with alcohol. I eventually chose to seek Jesus, in dealing with my anger and I let Jesus take control over it. Angry people say, and do angry things. Words do hurt, and they cannot be taken back. Ephes. 4:26: "Be ye angry and not sin.". One day, A. C. and I had dental work done by an old white male dentist in a downtown Chicago, office. The nasty geezer grabbed my derriere. I froze. A. C. very politely told me that he was upset, because I said nothing. I did not tell him that I thought he should have defended me. I had to work on trusting the Lord, and giving Him fears I did not realize I had. Prov. 29:25: "The fear of man bringeth a snare; but whosoever putteth his trust in the Lord shall be safe." I also, had to work on defending myself, when it came to old men.

I worked full time and attended various colleges, full time or part time, while married to A. C. One day, A consultant from Washington(LB), handed me a blank check, told me to fill in the amount, and asked me to move to Washington with him. He said; he would put me through school. I would have my own apartment and car. I did not want to leave my husband, and I surely was not planning on being a whore. Trust and believe L. B. had many women. However, I left A. C. and moved in with a male friend for a while. I did not want to take part in my new room-mates sexual play. A. C. lost his job. I moved back with him, and accepted the responsibilities of all of our living expenses. He had helped me take care of one of my substance addicted siblings for a while, and he had been a good provider. I owed it to him. He had a caring heart. I knew he messed around, but I overlooked it. I somehow believed he still loved me. I believed he would change, and become loyal to me. Yet neither of us were loyal to, Jesus.

I unfortunately got involved with cocaine. It helped me to stay awake for a long period of time. However, I felt the wicked one was taking over my soul. One day I went to meet an associate, just as I was getting out of my car, I saw policemen, leaving the building. Someone told me he/she had just been executed, and all of the drugs and jewelry had been stolen. AC, and I were behind in all of our bills. He was an unemployed nickle and dime player. I started feeling worn out. I was tire of this life. Our rent was too far behind for us to catch up, on. My income alone was not enough. So, A. C. and I eventually moved in with Motherdear. Grand-daddy had gone home to glory, about ten years earlier. One of my siblings and his family were already living there. I chose to change my life. No one in my family had ever helped me do anything. I took advantage of this opportunity to discontinue my indulgence with cocaine. I wanted to never be addicted to anything other than Jesus. Jesus, lead me and A. C. , helped me accomplish this goal. 1 Corint. 16:15: "they have addicted themselves to the ministry of the saints." I took Jesus and my bible into my bedroom for six weeks. I came out, addicted to Jesus, only.

One evening, my sibling came in my living area with a hanger, hanging on his penis and a shirt hanging on the hanger. How gross is that? I told his wife. However, she knew about his misbehaviors prior to marrying him. He did not deny this. Another day I saw him upstairs inappropriately attired, in the presence of both of my nieces. I told his wife and reported him. I told them I did it. They were furious with me. After thirteen years of marriage, at 33 years old, I decided to put my academic endeavor(s) on hold. I believed I was mentally and emotionally healthy enough to start having babies. Time was not waiting for me. I was getting old. I had always wanted a boy, girl, and then another boy. A. C. and I prayed to God for a baby boy. Especially when praying, A. C. had awesome and mannerable communication skills. I have come to realize that at that time I communicated like my parents, always hollering and screaming when I got upset. I often thought that was why A. C. , did not like me. A1 was born after 13 years of marriage; and we had prayed and cried out to, God to bless us with a son. I had been in labor for twenty three hours, before delivering him. I had to be induced. The doctors said he had to be born within twenty-four hours.

A. C. , had never been dedicated to me. I was not sure if I loved him anymore. However, I wanted my dream family. I asked him if someone gave him the option of $5K or me, which would he choose? He chose the money. To think, I gave up a blank check from a millionaire for him. Wow! A. C. told me he wanted A1, but not me. I would not let him have our baby.

A1 was born on one of my sibling's birthday. His wife said, she would never be able to top that. I flip this wicked spirit of jealousy, in the name of Jesus. A few months after A1 was born he was collicky for at least three months. He cried so much one night until he kept gasping. My sister insisted he was having breathing problems and wouldn't rest until we took him to the E. R. The doctor laughed at me. I too, laughed with my sister. She insisted a doctor was going to see him, until she heard the doctor say that he was okay.

I was working and saving money to get us an apartment. Although I paid my mother to babysit, money could not pay for the love she showed him. My family and I walked the floor with him. While I was at work, they were in the emergency room or doctor's office with him. We loved him through it. Then he had to have a cyst removed from behind his ear, and he developed pneumonia. We loved him through that. We loved him through anything and everything we thought hurted him. During his fight with pneumonia, I worked during the daytime and the hospital allowed me to sleep on a cot in his room, every night; until he came home. A. C. was no where to be found. I was sleeping on my parent's couch before finding us an apartment , so A. C. would move with us. A. C. said he did not want to live with my parents. A1 was wonderful. I walked from east 93rd St. to West 98th St., and back (approximately 3 miles), almost every day. While we enjoyed our time together, A1 was quietly and observantly relaxed in his Mercedes of strollers. He was so reserved and laid back. He was walking by nine months old, and potty trained by eleven months old. At approx. sixteen months old, I took A1 for his immunization and he was lead poisoned. I was told he was (2)two points from death. He endured two weeks of chelation not once but, twice two weeks apart. We both were crying before arriving to the clinic. He had a nurse who was there for every treatment, the first time. The second time, "Jackie", said she could not go through it again. She said it was extremely painful for him. I was not allowed to accompany him. I was told I wouldn't be able to deal with it. A. C. chose not to go to any of the appointments. I did not feel alone. I consistently prayed. I knew Jesus was with us. The doctor told me: I had to have him at the clinic at exactly 8am every morning, in order to keep him home with me. The only other option was to hospitalize him. We got on the CTA bus and arrived to the clinic every morning at exactly 8am. I knew Jesus was with us both. Hebrew

13:5 "For he hath said, I will never leave thee, nor forsake thee." A1's screams were excruciating. They penetrated my heart. I sometimes still hear him when reminiscing. So, you know back then, I was crazy with pain, fear, sympathy and empathy. I contacted the city to inspect our apartment. Lead based paint was everywhere. It had been covered by wallpaper. The owner of the building died a couple of weeks later, and no lawyer would help us pursue this. After all we lived on 93rd and Rhodes, in one of the better neighborhoods. I found out that the majority of the apartments in Chicago had lead base paint on the walls.

One of my siblings lived in Northern

Michigan, and told me I would be able to get affordable housing here. I had us packed in two days. However, I had a debt to pay. You see, when I was a little girl, a neighbor across the street from my parent's house had, on many occasions donated her daughters over used clothes to me. I was grateful to get the used and sometimes tattered socks, undies, pants, skirts, and(or) etc. . They were better than nothing. Anyhow, before we left town, she asked; for A1's nicely kept stroller. I felt like I owed her. I thought A1, no longer needed the stroller so, I let her have it. It felt awesomely wonderful, to pay that debt. I believed she was being evil by giving me things that were not suitable for her child. The good out of this is; I learned to never give other people things that's not good enough for me. I remember her sitting in her window with binoculars and looking into our house. I disliked her intrusion. I felt violated. Regretfully, I reacted by giving her the middle finger or dancing in our window. Years later, I apologized and she gave me a bad reference on a job I had applied for.

It was now November 1991. I had saved $4k. I packed us in two days, and left for Michigan. My sister's husband, M. A. was headed back to Michigan. I paid one of my siblings and his friends to load the U-Haul. I paid M. A. to drive us there. RIP, M. A. In 2006, he had a heart attack, and died. After arriving in Northern Michigan, I hurried and found a place. My sister told me she was not happy and was planning to move back to Chicago. I had to get Mental therapy because of the problems done A1, by the lead poisoning. Unfortunately A1, had regressed in his development, had a learning disability, and symptoms similar to ADHD. I enrolled him in ISD for four years.

Dt. 33:27: "The eternal God is my refuge." My therapist said; it was like the experience of losing a child, and the birth of another one. He was definitely a different

A1. In 1805, sixty-six years prior, Detroit had been destroyed by fire. History had been repeated. I researched and found out that after the great Chicago fire, Chicago was rebuilt with damp wood that had been shipped from Michigan. The only paint that took to damp wood, was lead based paint. My sibling shortly thereafter moved back to Chicago. A1 and I stayed. I asked; A. C. to come with us. He refused. Every day for two years I chased the school bus to Mason Lake-I. S. D. The staff told me he would never be able to talk articulately, or learn. I told them the devil was a lie and the truth was not in him. I told them, I wanted to teach A1 to tap in on that 73% of his brain that we do not normally use. They taught me how to teach A1. I became his main teacher. I learned many things and later worked as a part time, on call paraprofessional in the public school system. I loved working with children who had learning problems.

I again asked A. C. , to join us. I did not want my child to be hurt because of his dad. I should have known better. A. C. , had a daughter prior to our meeting. He ignored her. I use to try to get him to spend time with her, until her mother one day to my surprise, jumped on me. She told me; she was upset because, she wanted A. C. to marry her instead of me. A. C. thought her attacking me was funny. It wasn't but, it is sad that he missed out on getting to know two beautiful children. I was attending a church meeting and met G. M. He could preach and sing. He knew the Bible, but so does satan. I wanted a husband who loved, God. I believed this wolf in sheep clothing, did. A1 was now asking for a sister. I told him to pray. G. M. had been going around town asking about me, and trying to find out where I lived. One of his friends, moved all of his things to my house unannounced. They both told me they were only friends. I believed them.

I got pregnant and A2 was born, after carrying her for 10 months. I kept dilating at home but, by the time I made it to the hospital the dilation had gone down to zero(0) . This went on for a month. I was in consistent prayer. A1, G. M. , and I wanted this baby. Luke 11:9: "Ask and it shall be given." Earlier in my pregnancy I heard an older woman say; heated castor oil and orange juice would induce labor, if you are already in labor. If you are not in labor, you will have a good bowel movement. I chose to try it. I am not, I said I am not advising anyone else to try this.

One evening the Holy Spirit told me I was going to lose her. I had to help her. I was losing her! I was losing my babygirl! I became frantic. I prayed and drank the before mentioned solution. She was born about 4 four hours later. Dr. G. said; she is only here because God, wants her here. She was the cutest and most adorable baby girl, I have ever seen. Her name means the angels are always leaning over her. A1 and one of my siblings went to the hospital with me. G. M. wanted to be there, but I left him. He said; he had a previous experience of watching his child being born, and it grossed him out. He hated the sight of the baby coming out of the vagina, and would not touch the mother after that. I did not want to go through that, with him. After all, I wanted one more boy. I had called one of my siblings. She came from out of state. She was always in the room with me when I had a baby. She is braver than me. The hospital was not going to misplace my baby, with her there. When A1 saw A2, his face lit up like a christmas tree. He said, "She is so beautiful". It was love at first sight. I could have made a million dollars off of his smile, had I taken a picture. Approximately a week after she was born, G. M. , said he was going to be the first to have sex with her when she got about fourteen. Whenever I reminded him of that remark, he said he was joking. I never slept when he was around. I could not trust him. I told him I was going to do life in prison, if he touched her. Yet, nothing soothed me when he was around. I could not stand for him to touch me. Anyhow, after she was born and, due to the lack of oxygen she received in the latter month of my pregnancy; her eyes were bloodshot red for a year. However, she had no brain damage, and has always been academically above she and A1's peers.

We had moved into a house I decided to buy. Come to find out the house is built on Indian burial ground. It is haunted and had lots of noisy energy going on inside of it. Another stressful reason to sale it. I wanted a boy, girl, boy, and decided G. M. could be the sperm donor. He did not have to live with us. Yet, he refused to leave.

A1, started asking for a brother. I told him to pray. Before I knew it, I was going into labor with A3. As soon as my body started the labor process, I drank the heated, Castor Oil and Orange Juice. Again, I am not advising anyone else to try this. He was here within 4 four hours. A Nurse told me I had uterine inertia. My body would start , but not complete the labor process. This explained why Mother-dear carried eight babies full time, and all were steel born, except for mamma. Anyhow, A3 was born.

I took A3, in for his first immunization at two weeks old, the doctor went to give him a shot and he screamed, "Mammaaaaa." The doctor said; she would not have believed it had she not seen it for herself. A1 next asked for a house full. I told him to stop praying. I was done having babies. I lost a baby, and then got my tubes cut. I promised God that I would help his children who are already here. I am sure you guessed by now, that I ignored the warning signs , of G. M.'s, deceitfulness and fell into his trap. I saw the man he could be. Not the man that he truly was. I believed I could change him. I also, figured by the time A2, reached 14 years old I would have left him, if I was still alive. Prov. 12:20: "Deceit is in he heart of those that imagine evil: but the counsellors of peace is joy." I promised myself; I will not raise another woman's grown son who I am interested in as a mate.

Two other women had babies by G. M. He used the children in his wicked schemes by keeping them apart from one another. Regardless to what he and the mothers said, or did I have always told my children about their siblings. I do not believe children should be involved in an adult's ignorance. G. M. had a son born two months before A2 with the before mentioned friend and, another son born two months after A2. A3 was born one year and three months after him. I found out the hard way, what a wolf in sheep clothing is.

Two years later, I had a slip and fall accident when leaving the bank. I have been cripple every since. I had just left my job at the foster care home for the evening. G. M.'s, grandparents were entrepreneurs of that establishment. I was thankful for the job. I earned everything my children got. They did not get a Christmas, birthday present, etc. from G. M.'s, family that I did not work for. The day I fell I was extremely tired. The Holy Spirit, told me to go home, a few times. I argued with the Holy Spirit ; I just wanted to go for a short walk. I was disobedient and went for the walk. Trust and believe, my disobedience did not hurt God. I hurt myself. 2 Corinth. 2:9: "That I might know the proof of you, whether you be obedient in all things." This is what happened: I drove near the bank. I had parked across the street. I was on my way into the bank, to take care of my business. I slipped on some " black ice". It might have been black, but God, knew it was there. I chose not to listen to the Holy Spirit. I caused this to happen to myself.

I was a good mom. I tried very hard to make up for my children's biological family. I did not want them to feel as I had so many times. I did not want them to think that they did not have a parent who loved them. I worked two part time jobs. One at the Foster Care Home, and the other as an on-call Paraprofessional, at the local School. I kept my children and our house clean, and I played with my children. Before I became disabled, I taught A1 how to play basketball and how to defend himself. I was always interacting with A1, A2, and A3. If there was a supermom, I was she. Heb. 5:8: "yet learned he obedience." Yes, I have learned to be obedient.

The first time G. M. had come to my house, He asked me to marry him. I thought I would grow to love him. I did. I still refused to marry him for about six

66

years. I thought we were morally opposites. He did not talk to others as he wanted to be talked to, and he did not treat others as he wanted to be treated, just like some of his other family members. I plead the blood of Jesus over this generational curse of this evil behavior. May Jesus send them back to the burning fire of hell, where they came from. They can no longer exist in my lineage. All glory to, God!!! When G. M., returned from prison, he had changed.

After marrying him, I decided he had way too many other problems. I did not want my children or I to remain victims of his verbal, mental, and (or) physical abuse.

It took me many years, after G. M.'s death to intensely understand Ephes. 6:12 "For we wrestle not against flesh and blood, but against principalities, against powers, against the rulers of the darkness of this world, against spiritual wickedness in high places." Again, I plead the blood of Jesus, against any and all wickedness towards me and my lineage. 1 John 3:8 "For this purpose the Son of God was manifested, that He might destroy the works of the devil."

Due to the accident, I suffered terribly with my right knee. A doctor casked it and, it progressively got worse. I remember one day screaming at the top of my lungs and crying for hours. No other doctor would remove the cask. G. M. got us a ride and took me back to Fremont to the doctor who had originally put the cask on. The doctor kept saying he was too busy to see me. G. M. had a conversation with him, and he removed the cask. I had obtained a lawyer, who later said he could not take the case. I still did my best for my children. Over the years other physical problems have surfaced, because of my knee. As the pain grew out of control A1, A2, and A3, stepped up and took on responsibilities. They kept the authorities from taking them from me. No one helped us, not even our family. But everybody criticized me. I have always kept a neat house. Someone started calling Child Protective Services, with lies. So, I started smoking premos to help me deal with the pain. I had to make sure my house was immaculate, and my children went to school. The doctors kept saying that they saw no reason for such severe pain. I was not going to let them set me up for failure.

A1 was very good at basketball. I pleaded with him not to stop playing. He said; his family needed him and we were more important than basketball. I was too sick to argue and did not have anyone else to help us. No matter who I called, I received no help with the children or household. I kept one of my televisions on TBN

24-7. The Holy Spirit, was my guidance. He constantly told me to take care of the three A(s). As a matter of fact, when each of them were born, I held them to heaven and gave them back to, God. Anyhow, my children would not allow anyone to change the station. The pain was so excruciating, they told me I used to moan and cry in my sleep, when I did sleep. The Holy Spirit, sometimes awakened me by calling my name, or pulling my toe, or touching my ear, etc. , always just in time to hear the answer to questions I had asked of, God. A message would be on T. B. N. , just for me. For example, I asked, how would I discipline my children? I was awakened to the understanding of using the rod. In biblical times the rod was used to protect and guide the sheep or pull them out of danger, not to beat them. Ps. 23:11: "thy rod and thy staff they comfort me.", Beating a child is not what is envisioned as good parenting. The rod and staff is the Bible and Jesus. .

The doctors still said they saw no reason for so much pain. One day, while I was talking with a lady from social security, she told me I needed to contact mental health. I did. I was given therapy, and Effexor A. S. A. P. My therapist said the pain was so high, I had become mentally imbalanced. I was sent to a bone surgeon. He asked me how did I not hurt myself or someone else. I told him Jesus took care of me. I had to get the pain under control. I remembered reading about president Kennedy getting daily shots of cocaine due to a severe back problem. I did not want anyone to take my children from me. The bone specialist said; I had tiny pieces of bones floating around in my Knee. I was placed on the appropriate medications, and discontinued self medicating. My children and I were told by the therapist to accept my early death. I have never seen my children so hurt, depressed, and angry. I told them that only God, can make that decision. This is when A1, became angry with God and really started acting terribly out of character

I told them to pray, and God would hear them. Acts 10:31: "Thy prayer is heard." That was fifteen years ago. I am growing more and more in God's mercy and grace. 1 John. 5:4: "This is the victory, even our faith." I told them to always hold onto Jesus', hand no matter what and we would always be together. Prior to therapy , they had each taken a responsible role in the house. A1, was a caring father figure. He was a very good non-abusive person. A2, was a strong fearless mother. She was very good at giving orders, and non violently enforcing them. And A3 , was like grand-daddy. He loved to cook and tried to be in control of us all. There were times when A1, prepared the grocery list, and when he asked me what did I want; I would say candy, cookies, ice cream, etc. A1, would tell me that I needed fruits and vegetables. He would take one of his siblings with him on the community's pay bus to the grocery store. A3, would sometimes sit a chair in the kitchen and have me sit and watch him bake. A2, made sure that I was not antagonized or easily aggravated by others. God had sent me three angels. They were positive in my healing process. However, I did not want to repeat my mother's mistake with me and rob them of their childhood. It was hard to get A2, and A3 to go to school every day. One of them was always trying to stay with me regardless to how much I protested. There were times when I was paranoid and made all of them sleep in the family room with me. I was prepared to protect them as God, had instructed me. When I was in that extremely defensive frame of mind, they would pray for no one to come to the door. God, answered their prayers each time. Everything was so dependent on me, and that old demon, fear was trying to take over. I remember one time my babies told me that I hadn't taken a bath in a few days. It was then that I knew I had problems. It was abnormal for me not to groom and take a bath, every day. If I never trusted anyone else, I trusted the three A(s). We had one another's best interest at heart. We were a team. Even though different bone specialists have performed a total of three surgeries, The problems continues to this day. After seeing the mental therapist, I believed my children needed more than I could give them. Who would love my children enough to take care of them, until they became old enough to take care of themselves? I had taught A1, A2, and A3 to tell, if ever someone touched them in the wrong places. I've tried to teach them to respectfully stand up for themselves, and not to be afraid to speak up for righteousness. We all have a strong dislike for abuse, especially sexual abuse. Anyhow, who would help my babies, if something happened to me? My children had been deprived of so much. I accepted, eventually fell in love with, and finally married G. M. , just to be disappointed. Yeah, well who was zooming who? I had to face the reality that we were better off without him. He dwelled on confusion, drama, and negativeness. We deserved better.

I started listening to my Holy Spirit, again I had to let go of that fear, and hand it over to Jesus. I believed Jesus would not leave me or my children destitute. G. M. acted like he thought he was a God. He had no regard to the nonproductive effect his actions were having on us. He was a menace to himself, us, and our community. As fast as I accepted his true choice of attitudes, I tried to get out of his entrapment. I do believe united you stand, divided you fall. A house, community, state nation and/or world divided against itself, will not stand. G. M. , and I were divided. I wanted to be an answer to the problem, not a part of the problem. He without a doubt, was a walking time bomb. Num 27:3 "died in his own sin." His mistreatment of others, years later influenced someone to murder him. Now that person is doing life. Mothers, fathers, children, spouses, uncles, aunts, and etc. are hurting because of someone's retaliation of another person's destructive behavior and attitude. G. M. had a couple of times, caused his own family to be threatened and shunned upon, instead of trying to keep us safe and being a positive christian leader for our family. His constant threats towards me kept me in fear of him for a long time. He would walk behind me, aggravating and embarrassing me in private and in public places. He stole money and anything else he wanted from me. Which means he was taking from our children. I was still their sole provider, and he was

preying on me. I sent a beautiful gold

diamond ring, bone gold necklace, and a

bracelet, via certified mail to Chicago to

keep him from stealing it. I wanted to

eventually give our children something

from G. M. To this day my mom denies

signing the return receipt. I wonder which

one of my siblings did she give it to. She

always took from me and kept my things,

or gave them to my siblings. This was at

the same time that one of my siblings ran

over her wedding ring and had to have the

diamond in it replaced (just a thought). To

add to the negative energy; G. M. , con-

stantly told me he was going to take all

three of our children from me. One of my friends A. S. , and I had to drive to his mistress (J. K.), house one day and retrieve two of our babies. He and his mistress wanted to have them for themselves. I could not get rid of him, even when he went and lived with his mistress. He enjoyed picking fights with me. One incident that really sticks out in my mind is; after G. M. had caused problems and turmoil at my home all night, he followed me to the children's school the next morning. He had been antagonizing me all night, and someone in a Suburban type vehicle drove around my house a few times. I blew up at him in front of the receptionist. She, protested (she was one of his police officer friend's wife.). I told her off, without cursing.

Later that day, within minutes of G. M. leaving my house after trying to force his way in, two police officers came knocking on the door. I was in pain, cripple, and could barely walk. I asked the officers could I hang up my phone, as I turned to hang it up. The officers pepper sprayed me, and took me to jail. They said; I resisted arrest. I was already having problems with truancy. The same receptionist, was marking my children absent when they were tardy. I called my mother and asked her to come and get my children, on the day of court. I had sold my house within two weeks prior to this incident. It was beautiful. I paid Habitat for Humanity off and whoever else I owed. I was told to plead no contest. I tried to explain to the judge the problem with truancy. He told me to go to jail, anyway. I was sentenced to 30 days in jail for truancy and resisting arrest, of which my court appointed lawyer had told me to plead no contest. I would consistently read my bible, pray, and sing gospel songs. Sometimes I sang the women to sleep. they heard the peace and love of Jesus, in the songs. I only sang gospel.

I was surprised and, thankful that my mother came and helped me. This was so important to me. Due to her, G. M. and his mistress did not succeed, in taking my babies. 1 John 5:14-15 "14. And this is the confidence we have in him, that if we ask anything according to his will, He heareth us: 15. And if we know he hears us, what-soever we ask, we know that we have the petition that we desired of him." I had asked God, not to let anyone take my babies from me. One thing that I loved about G. M. , is that he did not make a difference in our children. He said; he would love a dog , if it was a part of me. He loved A1, as much as he did A2, and A3. that meant alot to me. However, he was a lot meaner towards A3. He said A3 was just like him.

Dilla (Ree) Scott

None of us allowed him to mistreat A3. He really got mad at A3 one day because at approximately 6 years old A3 told me right in front him "mamma, daddy just ain't any good."

My babies and I moved to Chicago. We did not have much left, materialistically. G. M. , never helped buy anything. However, he sold everything he could, while I was incarcerated. He sold our furniture, appliances, clothes, pictures off the walls, and etc. I did not care. I had my babies. When I got out of jail, I stopped in Inkster. G. M. , tried to convince me he wanted his family. He took all of my money and held me there. I kept telling him I had to get our

86

children. He wanted them to come to us. I
have learned not to trust a man who
cannot accept the two letter word: N &
O=NO. I did not argue or fight. I stayed
in prayer, and waited for the right time.
Job 14:14 "I will wait, till my change
come."

I was trying to keep my children away
from abuse. I kept my bag packed. I told
him that is how I was able to keep up with
everything. We slept in his mother's base-
ment. I had stashed my bridge card. The
morning the money came on it, I was on
the bus to Chicago. Upon arrival, I embraced my children, siblings, and parents.
I had been lying to my children about my

make believe, Donna Reed Show family, for so-o-o-o-o long, until I had started believing my lies. I told my children, my family was nurturing. I had them believing my daddy would not hurt me, or let anyone else hurt me. The saddest part of all of this is that my children got hurt because of my lies. John 8:32 "And ye shall know the truth, and the truth shall make you free. " Now, I had to make sure the abusers did not hurt my children, no matter of the cost to me. While living in Michigan my children told me many times of how alone they felt by not being around any of their biological family. When I did take them to Chicago, My children were treated as if they were beneath their cousins. All my life, I had been treated as if I was beneath my siblings. I was told that I was the oldest girl, so I had to go without eating when there was not enough food for everyone, or wash everyone's clothes, or clean behind everyone, or get molested. I was told it was a Southern tradition for the first born girl to be given to her father. In all actuality, I was my parents sacrificial lamb. I suddenly felt the emotional urgency to get my children to a safer place.

While in a shelter in Chicago, one of my siblings came and told me; my dad was hospitalized. I cried because I wanted to fit in with my sibling. I thought that's what was expected of me. Still my children and I were rejected. Probably because, that sibling knew the truth about my dad. He knew the Secret Sin, and he wanted me to be his puppet on a string. However my not having to have a man living with me, to survive took power away from him. God ended many generational curses, by guiding me through the Holy Spirit, and blessing me with his grace. He was not going to allow anyone to abuse my children.

I now understand why the Holy Spirit guided me to pay my parents, $600. a month for rent as long as we were in their house. Daddy didn't think he was taking care of my children, and his narcissist spirit was defeated. Everything he did for me was at a price. God met his price. I wasn't planning to stay there very long. However, I wanted to be absolutely sure my children were safe. Daddy was constantly talking to me about the pass. He asked me to forgive him for molesting me. I told him I forgave him. He still had a filthy way of looking at me. He told me he forgave me for telling his secret. I am glad I told his secret. His secret sin, was not of, God. Daddy said; he promised Mother-dear he would keep momma from going to jail. When A. C. and I were staying with Mother-dear I told Motherdear, that daddy had molested me. When momma, told me what motherdear told her I became terrified like I had so many times in the pass. I immediately remembered as a child; everytime I came close to telling momma she would say that she would kill anyone who hurt her children. I still wanted no part of that. I stayed silent. Anyhow, memories of the molestations started coming back, while in Chicago. I started remembering things like: I was just a little girl, and he would make me sit on his lap and play with his penis. He would feel on my body, butt, breast, vagina, etc. every chance he got. He would make me go to the basement with him and make me lay on the basement floor on top of rags that smelled like the dog had urinated, regurgitated, and or pooped on them, while he took my body. (To this day, that odor nauseates me). Sometimes I have odor flashbacks, so I normally keep my favorite fragrance on me in order to soothe my sense of smell. Most importantly, I remember once I realized he had crossed the boundaries of a parents love, I promised Jesus, that I would not be anything like him. I was around ten years old when a light went off in my head, that he was abusing me. One day some girls in my fifth grade class were asking me, if I was a virgin or non-virgin. I asked them what did the words mean. They kept edging me on to pick either or. To fit in, I did. The girls then told me the meaning of virgin. It was a joke and they tried to get me to laugh with them. I was too embarrassed. I was devastated. I then promised to never touch anyone inappropriately. My children take that after me. We believe in Grand-daddy's saying; a man's word is his bond. I refuse to feel sorry for myself. Proverb 12:19 "Truthful words stand the test of time, but lies are soon exposed." I have kept my word. Whenever the wicked spirits try to make me feel sorry for myself or relive the tormented past of abuse done to me, I visualize Jesus on the cross and the abuse he underwent by the chosen people, Pilate, and the roman soldiers. Daddy was so proud of his pass actions and the control he had over us. He showed no remorse. He boasted about how no authority would help momma without his permission. I am proud Jesus, did not let that ugly behavior live in me or my lineage. I boast about Jesus' love, and everything he does for my children and me. Psalms 34:2 "My soul shall make her boast in the Lord." I make it a habit not to purposely hurt others. When I do realize I have done wrong to someone, I remorsefully ask that person and Jesus for forgiveness for exactly what I have done to hurt them, along this journey. Daddy said; his first wife said she had to divorce him to keep from killing him, because of his whorishness. I pray daddy is with, Jesus. During my return to Chicago, I had to come to the realization that daddy had molested three and possibly four generations of females. I told one of my siblings about one of his then recent escapades. A couple of evenings later, I was in the outdoor basement stairwell, and I heard a different sibling fussing at him about the occurrence.

I trust my children told me the truth that they had not been touched by daddy. While there, I made A2 and A3 sleep on the couch with me. A1 slept upstairs. My mother told me she did not want us in her house. I was exterminating and killing her roaches. We temporarily moved in with one of my siblings before going into the shelter mode. Every shelter we stayed at we had problems with Al's, disobedience. I once asked the founder of one of the shelters who was also, Queen of the Coptic faith; Mrs. K. to discipline him for me, because I was too physically ill to do so. She whipped him in front of the entire church. A1, got worse. We came back to Michigan to prayerfully keep him alive and out of the legal system. However, prior to our move back, daddy reminded me every chance he got of the ugliness of my childhood. He never mentioned anything he did good, for or towards me. He had such a filthy and nauseating way of looking at me. I knew he was not serious about asking for forgiveness for molesting me. Just the same, I am glad I forgave him. My forgiving him is for God and I, not daddy. John. 8:29: "do always those things that please Him." Ps. 149:4: "For the Lord taketh pleasure in his people."

When daddy told me he forgave me for not keeping his secret. I wanted to do something evil to him. I did not explode because, I needed to gain insight by listening. Neh. 9:17: "Slow to anger." He was so proud of his actions. He showed no remorse. He was very proud of the control he had over us. He said; my mother could not get help from the authorities without his approval. He had to approve for us to get everything, including welfare. Many times after the beatings, momma would say he was sick. After listening to him talk, I believe he was nothing but an arrogant, self justified maniac. I was maybe ten years old when she encouraged me to sign daddy's name perfectly. All of us children, got new clothes with a Montgomery Wards credit card, momma made me sign for. Daddy went ballistic. He made me promise, to never again sign his name to anything. I kept my word. Everything we got from him, was earned through his molesting me, and beating momma. Daddy thought he was buying my soul. In all actuality, he was selling his own soul to the devil. By the age of 33 I had read many books written by positive advocates. The Bible has been my favorite, and it has been my eternal guide. I have been daily surrendering all the poison of pain and hate caused by my abusers to, God. Jesus and Grand-daddy are awesome. Jesus died for me, and adopted me into his family. Granddaddy reinforced everything about Jesus. For example, Granddaddy combed my hair, bathed me, fed me, and loved me unconditionally. He treated me the way he wanted to be treated. He talked to me the way he wanted to be talked to. He never hit me, or any other woman (that I knew about). He worked hard as a chef at Walgreens and even harder at being a good grandfather. He was quiet and mild-mannered. I had very little communication with my father's parents.

As I before mentioned, by the age of fourteen, I was working summer jobs. I was a hard worker. I earned money to buy school supplies and clothes. After graduating from high school, I put myself through college. I always worked full time and went to college full time or part time. I wanted to see how good I would do, if I really applied myself. I was on the Dean's list List while attending DeVry Institute of Technology. I normally kept a 3. 0 while attending Mundelein Women's College, and I also attended Northeastern. Finally , I did not have to miss school to care for my siblings, or I wasn't too bruised or hurt from the beatings, of which I would end up with black eyes. I was brainwashed into believing they were black because of anemia. It was in approximately 2008 that a doctor told me my eyes are black from constantly getting hit in them. My eye vessels were permanently damaged. I now call my eyes my battle scars. I try to stay away from confrontations (smile). When in grammar School my peers teased me and talked about my eyes. One of their names for me was, "Raccoon."

We moved from Ada to Morgan Park. We had moved to a better area of Chicago. We were the poorest family in the neighborhood. Most families consisted of two or three children. There was a total of twelve of us. My daddy had three boys and one girl by his first wife. He had four boys and four girls by my mom, of which I was the oldest girl. The kids in our community were always dressed better than me. I don't remember ever seeing any of them bruised or hurt. Most of them were bullies and were mentally abusive towards me. They were always pointing at me, while belittling me. Yet, I loved school.

There are two things no one can take from me, #1.) Jesus, and # 2.) My knowledge. The first thing we did every morning was to say, The Lord's prayer. Mat. 6:9-13 9:. "Our Father which out in heaven, Hallowed be thy name . 11. Thy kingdom come. Thy will be done in earth as it is in heaven. 12. Give us this day our daily bread. 13. And forgive us our debts as we forgive our debtors. 13. And lead us not into temptation, but deliver us from evil: For thine is the kingdom the power and the glory, forever." I felt like no matter what others said or did to me I had my Father in heaven watching over me, and he would handle everything, even the bullies.

The bullies called me everything, but a child of God. I did not need them for confirmation of God's, love and each day I forgave them. The Lord's prayer kept me from holding animosity. Anyhow, I just had my piano lesson. My teacher, D. F. gives me a sticker on the page of each accomplishment. I felt Ree's joy. It took me a couple of weeks longer to get the beat of "Blessed Assurance." That little girl who God has protected, and loved for so many years, was overjoyed with happiness. She clapped through me. She laughed, and smiled. She is finally letting me see her. 1John "We love him, because He first loved us." Ree, is finally getting a fulfillment of one of her dreams. Yay!! Today Ree, smiled. When I was a little girl, I used to dream of winning awards for dancing, singing, and playing the piano for, Jesus. Until recently, I had forgotten about these dreams. Anyway, Before M. J. and I married, we went to my first house party. The objective was to raise money for the hosts brother who was falsely imprisoned. I danced, won first place, and donated the money to their cause, as I had asked of God, before going to the party. My daddy was a very good dancer. Dancing is the only other behavior he had that I know God, likes. 2 Sam. 6:14 "David danced before the Lord." In 2006 my children and I moved back to Northern Michigan. I stayed with a friend who constantly said; she hated teenage boys. I hurried up and rented the first house I found. Unfortunately the landlord was a slumlord while receiving Section Eight grants from HUD. It was supposed to be temporary. I was afraid for my children's safety. The mold throughout the house was a safety issue. Soon after, My friend T. H. and his daughter followed us here from a shelter in Chicago. T. H. was a good team player. He was a hard worker. However, I did not notice until they moved with us, what I perceived as abnormal behavior towards his daughter. He got arrested and had to go to jail for a couple of months. I made arrangements for her return to her mom. He was mad. He said my accusations were wrong. He one day got drunk and said she was his _ _ _ _ _ and his meal ticket. The truth normally comes out when someone is drunk. He and my slumlord became very close friends. She stopped during much needed work on the house she rented to me. My home was found to be unlivable, by the authorities. My children and I moved further north to Cadillac. T. H. convinced me that I was wrong about his actions towards his daughter and he said; my ex-landlord's children would never let him be with her. I forgave him for his past disloyalty. I was not perfect. I deceived a church leader. I loved his biblical knowledge. However, I did not want to be with him. I do not date married men. I also, did not like his advice to me to; to give up on A1. Yet, he did not give up on his son. He said; A1 was a follower. We are all followers. I chose to be obedient to Jesus, and go after A1.

I felt the need to test him. So, I lied and told him I had always had feelings for him. I told him I loved sex. G. M. , taught me that if you tell someone something that you've not told anyone else, and it comes back to you, you know you cannot trust that person. I would have stopped him, had he come onto me. I knew he only liked light complexion females, so I was safe. I wanted to tap in on his wisdom, and had to find out if he could be trusted. He told me one sin lead to another. He also, told another church member. I know because, that member told me in the presence of other church members. The leader was not as wise as I thought he was. A couple of years after moving further north, I let T. H. visit. During his visit A2, told me she had something to tell me after he left in the morning. She promised he had not touched her. The next morning after he was far gone, she told me that he said; he wanted to see her in her night gown. He wanted to be the first to have sex with her. He said he would be careful, and not hurt her. I wanted to hurt him. I have told any man who tried to talk with me not to mess with my children. It took two weeks of crying and deep prayer to stay focused. I had to accept the fact that had I not committed fornication, this would not have happened. 1 Corinth. 6:13 "Now the body is not for fornication, but for the Lord; and the Lord for the body." It was not only the physical man that I was attracted to. It was always the spiritual man I knew my mate was capable of being. I came to realize, I can not make a man be who he does not want to be. Therefore, I must be aware of, and accepting of who a man is spiritually when confronted to start a friendship. I can only change myself. I cannot change another human being.

I promised A2, I would not react violently. You know, I would not like, bash his head in. When I confronted T. H. , he blamed the way he talked to my baby girl on his substance use. I asked God for forgiveness and practiced not being weak to lust. I am human, but I want to be a better person for God, myself, and my children. I moved to Cadillac, to give my children a better life. Yet I understand why the average African American/Multi-racial person only came to Cadillac to attend school or shop. They were not trying to live here. I pray parents start realizing that when they teach their children hate, that hate comes back to them. We have experienced quite a bit of racism. A2 was called "nigga bitch," "and all kinds of racist names, while sitting in the front of the school bus. When getting off the school bus, the same kids kept belittling her. The Bus Supervisor's, solution to the problem was to put her to the back of the bus. A3's elementary school principal addressed all bullying and racism issues. I met with the superintendent of schools and eventually N. A. A. C. P. about my concerns. When A3 began attending the Middle school, he was constantly having racism problems. One day a group of white boys surrounded him and called him racist names while attempting to fight him. A teacher pinned A3, to the wall and was choking him. A3, was struggling to get loose. He said; he could not breath. Instead of the principal addressing the issues of bullying, he was engulfed in pornography. The Civil Rights Commission and N. A. A. C. P. had a meeting with the board. The school had affirmative action classes, because my children stood their grounds, A3, wrote various black celebrities, but no one even encouraged him. He wrote Disney World, and received a nice T-shirt. The Cadillac Schools eventually had diversified training classes. Neither my children or I, were made aware of the classes. I just so happened to find out about the class(es) a year later. Nothing had changed. one of A2, classmates told her he wanted to burn a cross in a black person's yard. Although this was reported to the school, they did not do anything. As A3, has so often said: and we have a black president. Obama, was now the first black president. I told him that even Obama, had to go through something to get to where he is. Most of A1's, classmates ignored or rebelled their parents teachings of hate and racism. They talked about their feelings on the subject when they came to our home. I came to analytically believe, the bullies found temporary peace through drugs, and the bullied turned to suicide. Only Jesus, can give us eternal peace. Back to Alex, accidentally hitting the teacher while struggling to get free from the choke hold on his neck. He told me he kept trying to tell the teacher he couldn't breathe. When he did get loose, he ran to the streets and called me from his cell phone, that the staff did not want him to have. I was on the highway, on my way from a doctor's appointment. I did 85 instead of the lawful 70 mph to get to him. He was on the road alone and upset. I did not see a teacher or anyone else in site. The authorities would not allow me to press charges against the teacher. However, charges were brought against A3. On the day of court, prior to entering the courtroom the state police officer took the witnesses in a room and talked to them. The boys got on the stand and lied. . A3 was expelled. Sometime later, one of the boys sent A3 an apology for lying in court. I taught my children not to hold grudges, but to forgive and let God, handle the situation and we can use the memories as a testimony to help others.

A2 and A3 said they did nothing wrong, and they did not want to move. Although A3 had attempted suicide on two different occassions due to the bullying, of which each time the Holy Spirit sent me to inter-vene, I stood their grounds with them. We did not move. Alex, promised me, he would never again attempt suicide. Mark 12:31 "Thou shalt love thy neighbor as thyself." Bullying is not of God, and It is not a way of expressing love. Suicide is the only sin you cannot ask for forgiveness for, after the sin has been committed. I have taught my children to hold onto Jesus' hand and we will all be together with Jesus, when the trumpets blow and we are called home to glory. Alex, knows a man's word is his bond. Suicide is a self centered, evil, wicked, and selfish spirit. When I was a little girl, I too had contemplated suicide many times. The hate towards me was too powerful for me to contend with. Praise God, that demon wasn't too powerful for, Jesus. I like to believe Jesus sent it back to hell to burn in the brimstones of fire with, Satan. It is power in Jesus, to anoint ourselves with Holy oil, and to plead the blood of Jesus, on oneself. 1 John 4:20: "If someone says, "I love God, " but hates a Christian brother or sister, that person is a liar; for if we don't love people we can see, how can we love God, whom we cannot see?" A2, listened to me. She chose to be home schooled for a while. A1 and A3 very seldom did as I told them, so they have had more problems than necessary.

As a matter of fact the caucasian lawyer who was representing A2 and A3 for a lawsuit due to racism quit because, he said; A3 always took matters into his own hands instead of telling us and letting us handle the issues for him. None of the three have adhered to the importance of a college education, as of yet.

After living in Cadillac for a while, and due to the change in my financial format, It became almost impossible for me to take care of my family. I had applied for Section Eight (assistance through H. U. D.), in 2006. I received it in 2011, months after I had returned home from being incarcerated. The death benefits we received from

G. M. was not extranomical, but every bit helps. We were living in a shelter in Chicago when G. M., was killed. His mom said; he had purchased a house and fixed it up for us. Two weeks before we were to move with him, he was murdered. It was years later when his dad told me that he had not changed. I could not get the boys to understand I could not afford to feed and support their suppose to be friends or girlfriends. Some of which just took advantage and moved into my house. Anyhow, I had grown tired of my children being deprived and, I wanted them to have a better life than I did. Also, saying "no", was not a part of my vocabulary when it came to my three children. As a child, although I was deprived of many things, because I was not allowed to say "no". I did not understand the importance of saying "no" to my children. So, I bought and sold a substance at a profit, in order to keep them from suffering any type of abuse. When I realized the drug could be deadly, I stopped selling it. However, I did not come to this realization prior to my unknowingly being set up by an informant whom I had become intimate with, and I decided I did not like him. I was arrested six months after I had changed. A1 had become intimate with a beautiful stripper/drug user, and started using. Again, no matter how much I protested, he moved her into my house against my wishes. When we were teenagers, we dare not sleep in let alone move into a boys mother's house, having sex over her head. Ephes. 6:1 "Children, obey your parents in the Lord; for this is right." Children should not have to be beaten, in order to do as they are told. In the long run your disobedience hurts you.

One night before I was incarcerated, I held my oldest child- A1, in my arms while he went through withdrawals. He convulsed and jerked. It was one of the worst experiences I have ever gone through. Mt. 6:24: "No man can serve two masters." I had served God first! all of these years, and I now was acting like my children were gods, Dt. 31:16-18: "and this people shall rise up and go a whoring after the gods of the strangers of the land, whither they go to be among them, and will forsake me, and break my covenant which I have made with them. 17. Then my anger shall be kindled against them, and I will hide my face from them, and will forsake me, and they shall be devoured, and many evils and troubles shall befall them, so that they will say in that day, are not these evils come upon us, because our God is not among us? 18. And I will surely hide my face in that day for all the evils which they shall have wrought, in that they are turned unto other gods." and I was not fellow-shipping with other believers. 1 Jn. 1:7 "But if we walk in the light, as he is in the light, we have fellowship one with another, and the blood of Jesus Christ his Son cleanseth us from all sin."

I asked; Jesus, A1, A2, and A3 to forgive me, and I repented. Yet, the process of reconciliation can be long and hard. Luke 6:37: "forgive, and ye shall be forgiven." The hardest person to forgive is , self. I had never been away from my children. I hit rock bottom by not keeping my heart on Jesus. Joshua 1:8: "This book of the law shall not depart out of thy mouth;

but thou shall meditate therein day and night, that thou mayest observe to do according to all that is written therein: for then thou shalt make thy way prosperous, and then thou shall have good success." I had strayed away from my Lord. I had put worldly desires before, God. 1 Tim. 6:10" "For the love of money is the root to all evil." My desire to give my children a better life than I had, became my goal. Deut. 6:16: "Ye shall not test the Lord thy God." I went to jail. I used the time I was incarcerated, to have an intimate relationship with God. Luke 13:3: "I tell you, Nay: but, except ye repent, ye shall all likewise perish." I did all the biblical studies offered, and received many certificates, and a bible with A1, A2 and A3 names on it, through Forgotten Man Ministries. The Bible got lost. If the grade of each temptation was not 100%, I talked with one of the administrators. I wanted to be sure of what I was learning. Gal. 6:7: "Be not deceived; God is not mocked:, for whatsoever a man soweth, that shall he also reap." I should have known better. 1 Thes. 5:6: "let us watch and be sober." 1 Peter 4:7: "Be ye therefore sober, and watch unto prayer."

A couple of months after my incarceration, I was placed in isolation because one of the young white female inmates did not want to hear me sing about, Jesus. The same corrections officer overdosed me, a couple of days later. Oh, but God, had a couple of His angels on duty that night, and because of their actions I live to glorify my, Lord. 1 Samuel 2:9: "the wicked shall be silent in darkness." One night, a few months prior to my release, two women got into a fight. It sounded like they were pounding one another's heads into the cinder block walls. The guards did not respond to the hollering. Before I realized it, I was intervening. I received a broken shoulder. Although I suffered with severe pain, I soothed myself by reminding myself that no one had died from the incident. My greatest accomplishment ever, was that on two separate occasions a woman accepted Jesus as her saviour through me. It is a wonderful feeling to know two souls have been saved, because of my disobedience to God, which caused my incarceration and initiated my meeting them. From those two souls, hundreds, thousands, possibly millions will be saved. Psalms 34:2 "My soul shall make her boast in the Lord." All glory to God. I never forced my Jesus on anyone, ; women would come to me to hear and talk about God, Jesus, and the, Holy Spirit. Praise God, The Holy Spirit, used me as his vessel. I was not in a room at home introvertedly, not sharing God, and keeping Him to myself. Upon my release, I was able to have surgery on my shoulder. I searched for a lawyer. I could not find one who would take the case. Mat. 16:26: "What is a man profited, if he shall gain the whole world, and lose his soul? or what shall a man gain in exchange for his soul?" During my incarceration, A1 went to prison, A2 stayed with another family, and A3 ended up in a group home, because no one would take him. As of 2007, he has been extremely sick with diabetes. He is possibly is a victim to Abilify, as a matter of fact, in 2013 he was in the hospital due to his diabetes and a doctor socked him. I was told the doctor would be reprimanded. However, no lawyer agreed to take the case. I believe Psalms 34:21 "evil will slay the wicked." The wicked spirits are running rings around my sons. On two different occasions, regardless to how much I protested A1, chose to take the blame and do time for female's unlawful behavior. He did not see himself as enabling them, or as setting himself up for failure. Upon A1's, release, he was harassed by the probation office. He was numerously falsely violated and lost jobs. A couple of times he was fairly violated and sent to T. R. V. , or whatever his P. O. decided to do with him. This last time, he was drunk and approx. 6 young men jumped on him. He was falsely accused of fighting an officer. Instead of sending him to rehab again, as the probation office had normally done caucasian people who violated due to substance abuse, A1 was sentenced to prison. I have heard certain nationalities should not consume alcohol. A1 is African, Creole, Indian, Haitian, Caucasian, Jamaican, and this is what I know of. I believe alcohol is totally against him. Anyhow Upon appeal A1, proved his innocence. The judge said since he had gotten into a fight in prison, he had to do the time anyway. He had gotten into a fight because, he had gotten jumped on and had to defend himself. Had he not been wrongly imprisoned, he would not have had a fight in prison. The man he fought was put on a higher level, and he was placed in lockdown. Because it was self-defense A1, was placed back into general population, early. I do not know what he has had to go through. However, I did tell him to stay to himself and go to church.

My daddy died in July of 2012. At the wait, I was standing over the casket, and it felt like I was being pulled in. I believe it was a wicked spirit. A2 grabbed me and pulled me towards her. During the funeral, While everyone else was crying out of grief, I cried with joy that he could not intrude on anyone else, and because my siblings were hurt. I believe it was an angry wicked spirit that caused A2 to fall while at the funeral.

Upon my returning home, I tried to become a member of a group of women who have gone through abuse. I again felt ostracized. I quit the group, and I walked out. I have always had my God, with me and do not engage in self pity. I refuse to keep crying over spilt milk without faith that God, can heal me. I did not wait until I was fifty years old to fall in love with God. I fell in love with him while I was being abused. God, is my First True love. Psalms 122:6: "they will prosper that love thee." The group leader said because I am not vulnerable, either I was never abused or I am hiding my feelings, or I am not honest with myself, or I am exceptional. I believe I am exceptionally advanced in my healing, because I keep my hands in God's hands. Jesus, first loved me. Our love for one another has been healing me. There was a time when I would have been reactive to another person's negative words or actions. For example; I was in the 7/4/2015 Freedom Parade. I was in front with my christian group. One of the community pastor's told me to get behind his group. I immediately praised and thanked God, for reminding me of Jesus' walk to Calvary. Look at what they did to my,

Jesus. He was treated way worse than I was. They lied on him, they beat him beyond recognition, they spit and urinated on him. They did many cruel things to him. They called him everything but the son of God. He was treated less than human. Look at what they did to my Lord, and yet, he still chose to take those stripes on Calvary for you and I. Dr. Martin Luther King, Jr., once said; if a man has not learned something is worth dying for, his life is not worth living. Jesus, believed we were worth His life. Sounds like to me that Jesus, was his mentor. Jesus, taught me to remember what he has done for me, and to be a testimony to others. Ps. 119:24

"Thy testimonies also are my delight and my counsellors." John 5:39 "They are they which testify of me." I have chosen to believe in Jesus healing me of the pain of the abuses done to me. Isa. 53:5 "with His stripes we are healed." Ex. 15:26 "I am the Lord who heal thee." Ps. 56:9 "This I know, for God is for me." Jn. 3:33 "God is true." I have always given him the pain and anger of the abuse, and I refuse to take it back. I am going to keep giving the pain to Jesus, as God, blesses me to let go of it. He gives me the healing, and I won't take it back. I will keep talking with him and giving him the painful memories as they surface. I will keep praying to progress in the glory of my Lord. Every day Jesus has been healing me from the torment of abuse. . . Isa 58:6 "Let the oppressed go free." I have to tell of my present landlord, T. D. He held his home for my family (for whatever reason), without receiving rent for nine months. He believed that I would pay him the money owed him regardless to what others said. I paid him every penny of rent, court charges, and late charges owed him, and I wish I could have given him more. T. D., is the second man I know to ever try to encourage my sons. Had he not had that house for me when I returned, I would have lost my then minor children. There was no help with housing available to a felon. He reminds me so much of my grandfather by the way he loves and respects his wife and family. Mr. D. has always kept my house and all of his rentals together in decent living condition. He's the complete opposite of a money hungry slumlord. He has showed me more Jesus love, in time of need than anyone I know. As usual, there was no type of support from any of our family. Thank you, Mr. D. The only other positive man that ever showed A3, any moral support was E. Totton. It broke all of our hearts when he lost his battle to cancer. Thanks to A3's baby's mamma mamma, he was sadly unable to be present for E. T.'s homegoing in 10/2014.

In July 2013, we had a family retreat, in Cadillac. Many of my family members came. We stayed the weekend in one of the best motels in town. We all had a blast. My oldest sibling, and his wife stayed a little longer and went to church with me. He has been texting me a biblical quote, every morning since that day. His messages are so on point, and supportive. God knows what we need better than we do. Today, 2/11/2014, Jr.'s Text; Ephes. 1:9-12: "9. Having made known to us the mystery of his will, according to his good pleasure which he has purpose in himself. 10. That in the dispensation of the fullness of times he might gather together in one all things in Christ, both which are in heaven, and which are on earth; even in him. 11. In whom also we have obtained an inheritance, being predestined according to the purpose of him who worketh all things after the counsel of his own will 12. That we should be to the praise of His glory, who first trusted in Christ."

I thank Jesus for holding me, for cradling me, baring my pain, for guiding me in the Holy Spirit, and crying for me, when a grown person who is suppose to be my protector put their grubby, filthy, stanky, non-tolerant hands on me. I thank Him for blessing me with the strength to hold onto His hand when I was beaten every time my mother looked at me and said I look like my dad. I thank God, for blessing me to accept being ostracized by my family, as long as my daddy was living. I thank God for being my mother, my father, my sister, my brother, my best friend, my husband, my everything. John. 7:37: "Jesus cried, if any man thirst let him come unto me and drink." Through the power of God, I have unknowingly, gone from being a victim to being a survivor of abuse. What God, has done for me, He will do for you. I pray everyone reading this book. has already, or will ask Jesus, into their heart. I pray you start going to a Jesus' blood pleading church, start reading the bible, and help others learn about the one who will save you, Jesus. Ree is revealing herself to me more, especially when children come around. Children love Ree. They normally draw to her. They laugh, and play with her. There was a time when a child came around, I had to take care of them. I have been telling my children for many years that I do not want to have to raise my grandchildren. I want to enjoy them, and send them home. I have never pushed a child away. I am called Grandma, by some of the children in the community. My first granddaughter was two years old when I first met her. I'll call her, A4. She has been consistently visiting us for a couple of months. I noticed that when she comes around, my chest doesn't hurt as much as it use to. Ree is happier. A4, comes around me because she has fun with me, not because she needs or wants me to take care of her. She is energetically independent. She has made a connection with someone she doesn't physically know; Ree. A4, does not need for me to take care of her. She loves to talk. Her mother is normally around or does not leave for long, Her mother loves being around her. Ree, is revealing herself all of the time, now. I first saw Ree during one of my therapy sessions with, Oasis. She stood in the middle of the floor with her back turned so I could not see her face. I wanted to take her out of my head. Yet, I recognized her. She is me. My first Christmas with, Oasis she asked for her own doll. She did not remember ever getting her own doll. Oasis, gave it to me for her. I let one of my friend's daughters play with it. Ree, exploded when the girl took her doll home without permission, and lost her socks and headband. I am a lot more apprehensive about my actions and decisions. I have chosen to accept and understand the child in me. I do not remember ever having a peaceful holiday. There was always fighting and confusion at my parents house. I don't remember ever getting a present that I wanted from them for Christmas. Sometimes, a few days just before the holiday, they gave me money of which I always spent on someone else. It was only one time that I did not spend all of it on my siblings. I see Ree crying for joy at not being afraid to reveal herself to me. I am learning not to put everybody before myself. Luke 13:29-30 "29. And, they shall come from the east, and from the west, and from the north, and from the south, and shall sit down in the kingdom of God. 30. And behold, there are last that shall be first, and there are first that shall be last." I will not always be last.

Ree is letting Dilla, into her world.

Now, Dilla and Ree, can start healing together. I know my therapist is happy with my progress. She loves to hear of my growth. Even though the devil, keeps trying to make me lose faith in my Lord; I keep holding onto his hand. This is a text From, Jr. Scott, my oldest sibling, on February 8, 2014, Isaiah 12:4-5. 4. "And in that day ye shall say, Praise the Lord, call upon his name, declare his doings among the people, make mention that his name is exalted. 5. Sing unto the Lord; for he has done excellent things; this is known in all the earth." One of my brothers passed while I was incarcerated. I cried because I loved him, not because I did something wrong to him or he did something wrong to me. We always told one another that we loved the other. Heb. 13:1: "Let brotherly love continue." There was no hidden secrets or regrets.

I have played the piano and sang over the phone to my mom and siblings. The walls are going down, since daddy's death. I am stunned at how quickly A4 freely shares her gigantic stuffed animal with me to play with. She shares with me because, she wants to; not because, she has to. I now realize, Ree does not like to share at all, right now. She especially doesn't like to share her doll. I am starting to realize I do not have to share everything. I know part of the healing is to not have or cause confusion within myself. I sometimes wonder where were my protector(s) when I was being abused. It's then that I have to remember my protectors were my abusers. Things get so painfully confusing, until I also remember Jesus, was there all of the time. 1 Corinth. 14:33: "For God is not the author of confusion, but of peace." Thank you, God: Jesus is healing me. For however long it may take, I have faith that Jesus is healing me. It is a blessing to know no matter what the world say about, or do to me; God loves me. In the name of Jesus, thank you Lord, for your mercy and grace. It is never too late to fulfill a dream, or to learn. I will be chasing my Jesus, for eternity. I have faith in receiving blessings from obeying, God. John 15:17: "Love ye one another." 2 Corinth 5:6-8 "6. Therefore we are always confident, knowing that, whilst we are at home in the body, we are absent from the Lord. 7. (For we walk by faith, not by sight:) 8. We are confident, I say, and willing rather to be absent from the body, and to be present with the Lord." I have been in consistent prayer with God, about the contents of this work in progress. He has assured me through Jesus, and the Holy Spirit, that I am not to be afraid of it's content. I am to testify of the truth, and bring His children to Him.

He has also conveyed edification and assurance to me of His, sending me into a world I knew nothing about, so that He could save His lost sheep. Luke 15:4 "What man of you having an hundred sheep, if he lose one of them, doth not leave the ninety and nine in the wilderness, and go after that which is lost until he find it?" God has brought me through so many trials and tribulations.

I now remember how my father's mother use to bring things into daddy and mamma's house and hide the object behind the cabinet, the refrigerator, anywhere she could when she thought my mother was not looking. Mamma would follow her steps, and find the object, she said it was voodoo, and would make me (her victim) throw it away. If any of the voodoo got on me I now give it to Jesus, to do what He wants with it. I was recently told that my father's grandparents were from Haiti. Again, I give those wicked spirits to Jesus, and I plead the blood of Jesus over A1, A2, and A3. I am now aware that wicked spirits have been attacking my family. Some are generational curses. God is rescuing us. The blood of Jesus, is my answer! The blood of Jesus, is your answer! The most recent incidents are very amazing, the final manuscript of "Secret Sin", was held up for a few months. Therefore, this is an insert: A3 has been hit and bullied by females in this community, who have not been taught to keep their hands to themselves. Not once was he allowed to press charges. I had told all three of my children numerous times to stay away from those who are trouble makers, mind your own business, Pick friends who are reaching for God, be careful of who you keep company with, use negative energy such as anger to do positive things like going to school and accomplishing a goal, do things to encourage other people instead of discouraging them, and discipline yourself not respond to negativeness with negativeness. Give the turmoil to Jesus, because he has already won the battle. You are the company you keep, so stay away from negative people. Everyone has to do what someone tells them to do. Even Jesus, did as God told him. We are not created to live alone. We owe it to God, to try to get along with one another. Think before we say and do anything, because in every action there in a reaction. I have always tried to be a positive parent for my children. A3 was always trying to be around his baby's mamma's family. Her step-dad an Indian, was constantly calling him a nigga and saying other evil things to him. He must hate himself because as I tell my children; you shouldn't hate what's in you. We as does the average African American/Multi-racial have, caucasian, Indian, etc., from our ancestry. Again, A3 would not listen to me. There's never been a camera in that police car before. They were aware of Alex's problem with diabetes and bi-polar. Did they set Alex, up for failure? One day his baby's mamma's, mamma attacked him and she got hurt. As usual A3, was not allowed to press charges. However, a few days later he was arrested. He wanted so much to be present when A5, was born. Here goes the reaction of the bipolar, and diabetes. He somewhat remembers breaking the camera stand in the police car. Why would they have anything like that in a place where it can possibly be broken by an arrestee? It sounds like a setup to me. After six months of sitting in jail, for destruction of police property, the judge at court told him if, he came before him again, A3 would go to prison. A3 had two more months to go. I believe someone wanted the judge to live up to his words. Did they set A3, up for failure. However, this is the same judge that sent A1, to prison even though he had proved his innocence. They knew how important his medications were for him. He is a brittle/reactive diabetic, and bipolar. His bipolar medication was taken from him aprox. 2 months after being incarcerated, and his insulin was not only changed by the nurse who I was told is a veterinarian, but he was also denied any insulin on two different occasions, which caused negative results. His brain quickly starts ketosis without proper regulation of his insulin. I made sure the probation officer, A3's lawyer, and the judge, were aware of his medical situation. Yet he was sentenced to prison (although I suggested a medical alternative). All of this because A3, did not listen to his mother and sister who stays in prayer for him and who loves him almost as much as, Jesus. I pray he has learned to listen to us. Mind you, before he went before the judge for a probation violation, fifteen days of his good time had been taken due to the same issue. I am standing in faith in the name of Jesus, that God will prevail. I don't believe that people realize in all of their self pride and control, that God, sees and judges the whole picture. I dare not judge. I know that is for God, to do. I plead the blood of Jesus, and repeat God's, words back to him over every situation past, present and future. I have prayed and am setting up blessings for my lineage. Isaiah 54:17 "No weapon that is formed against thee shalt prosper; and every tongue that shall rise against thee in judgement thou shall condemn." Gal. 6:7 "Whatsoever, a man soweth, that shall he also reap." and I pray for deliverance and God's children growth in him. Ps. 115:14 "The Lord shall increase you more and more. "I understand why God, blesses us to walk in the shoes of the one we are so insensitive to. We must learn to empathize and sympathize with one another. There's an old saying: By the grace of God, there could be I. You put out good seed, you get good back, and viceverse. I don't seek revenge because; Psalm 110:1 "The Lord said unto my Lord, Sit thou at my right hand, until I make thy enemies thy footstool." Our Lord's revenge is righteously justified. Jer. 15:15 "O Lord, revenge me of my persecutors." Nah. 1:2 "the

Lord revengeth, and is furious." Proverbs 16:7 "When a man's ways please the Lord, he maketh even his enemies to be at peace with him." I never rejoice in others failure. I pray our Lord has mercy on them, and that they realize their spiritual mistake and become closer with, God. Proverb 24:17-18 "17. Rejoice not when your enemy falleth, and let not your heart be glad when he stumbleth 18. "Lest the Lord see it and it displease him, and he turn away his wrath from him." Yet, my final and most important prayer is that God's, children come to know him. In the name of Jesus, I pray. I am so blessed to have taught A2, to keep her hands to herself. Most of us negroes/black people/African Americans/ Multi-racial people, normally teach our girls not to be justified bullies. Meaning; because you are a girl, you are not allowed to hit boys and boys are not being taught it's okay to be bullied by girls, and not to hit girls back. The bullying carries over into daycare and eventually into the schools and adds to the anger among students. A1, remains wrongfully imprisoned. Out of fear, Aryan nation inmates were motivated to fabricate a lie. They owed A1 some money (food). A1 was found to be inno-cent by the prison board. However, the judge and prosecutor took this as a politi-cal opportunity for votes to get the prison renovated or rebuilt. I depleted my savings on A1 and A3 legal fees. Oh, but watch God's video. I know God will prevail.

I believe the curse of all of this wickedness began when my parents chose to use me, their first born daughter as their, sacrificial lamb. In the name of, Jesus; As I forgive them and pray that they come to know Jesus, I forgive and pray for those who have chosen to use others as their sacrificial lamb, for political or any other reason. Flip it. I pray they all accept Jesus as their Savior, and as the one true and only Sacrificial Lamb. Although, during the trial I became somewhat confused about who A1's lawyer was representing, he did tell me he believes A1, is innocent. In the name of Jesus: I thank God, for blessing A1, A2, A3, myself, and all believers with the protection of THE BLOOD OF JESUS, and His Angels' Armies. I thank God for confirmation by the many sightings of Angels, lately. Some biblical researchers believe the sightings are signs from God. These beings are referred to as; heavenly angels, or celestials, or fallen angels, or aliens. I thank God for prophecy, for blessing His prayer warriors to consistently pray for us all, as well as each politician and the head of every nation. I thank Jesus, for intervening, for flipping evil intents, words and desires while sending wicked spirits back to where they come from. I thank my eldest sibling Jr. Scott, for daily sending me a scripture. They have been so encouraging. I thank my facebook family for being spiritually supportive. I thank God, for my Prophet Peter Popoff keeping me and my family on the altar of prayer, and for all of his spiritual support as we stand united in God, in prayer. Isaiah 50:8 "He is near that justifieth me." I have prayed many times that God blesses me as he did David, when he slew the giant. Bless me as he did Joseph after he was ostracized by his brothers. After many other tribulations, Joseph, as a leader forgave and received his brethren and father. Most of all I pray God forgives for each time as a little girl I considered suicide, and each time I am still a doubting Thomas, and had the faith of a mustard seed. I thank Jesus, and the Holy Spirit for spiritual strength, and guidance. God, will always prevail. The created will never be above the Creator. Isaiah 54:17 "No weapon formed against me shall prosper." I could never Praise God enough. Thank you Heavenly Father, in the name of Jesus. Amen! All blessings, and honor, to my Lord and Savior. Ephesians 6:12-17 "12. For we wrestle not against flesh and blood, but against principalities, against powers, against the rulers of the darkness of this world, against spiritual wickedness in high places. 13. Wherefore take unto you the whole armor of God, that ye may be able to withstand in the evil day and having done all, to stand. 14. Stand therefore, having your loins girt about with truth, and having on the breastplate of righteousness; 15. And your feet shod with the preparation of the gospel of peace; 16; Above all taking the shield of faith, wherewith ye shall be able to quench all the fiery darts of the wicked. 17. And take the helmet of salvation, and the sword of the Spirit, which is the word of God."

It's time to sing: "I'm on the battlefield for my Lord. I promised Him that I would serve Him until I die."

May God bless you and our lineage from our reading of His Holy Word. We must keep our hands in God's hands at all times. All glory to, God!!!

Following is the first song that I wrote to God, my true love. "In the name of Jesus."